WHEN WE BECAME
HUMANS
Our incredible evolutionary journey

Michael Bright

Illustrated by Hannah Bailey

words & pictures

Quarto is the authority on a wide range of topics.

Quarto educates, entertains and enriches the lives of our readers—enthusiasts and lovers of hands-on living.

www.quartoknows.com

First published in 2019 by words & pictures, an imprint of The Quarto Group. The Old Brewery, 6 Blundell Street, London N7 9BH, United Kingdom. T (0)20 7700 6700 F (0)20 7700 8066 www.QuartoKnows.com

Designer: Anna Lubecka
Consultant: Dr Laura T Buck
Editor: Emily Pither
Editorial Director: Laura Knowles
Art Director: Susi Martin
Creative Director: Malena Stojic
Publisher: Maxime Boucknooghe

A catalogue record for this book is available from the British Library.

ISBN 978-1-78603-886-9

Manufactured in Guangdong, China CC042019
9 8 7 6 5 4 3 2 1

MIX
Paper from
responsible sources
FSC® C008047
FSC
www.fsc.org

CONTENTS

WHAT'S A HUMAN?

Humans are unique. We grow crops, breed domestic animals and trade across continents. We talk and write with complex languages. We have the ability to reason, and we explore and try to understand the workings of the world. Art, music and literature celebrate what we see and hear. Complex tools enable us to construct buildings and create complicated machines, and we can even explore outer space. No other animal achieves all these things, but, like all animals, our evolutionary story has much simpler beginnings. In this book we explore the journey our ancestors took and the changes we went through to become humans.

So where exactly do humans fit in?

Hominids

Humans are also included with the hominids, or great apes. This is a subgroup of the apes that includes orangutans, gorillas, chimpanzees, bonobos and us, but not the gibbons.

Hominins

And, just when you thought scientists had invented enough words to describe humans, there's another one. Humans and our closest relatives are called hominins.

4

Mammals

Humans are mammals. Like all mammals, humans have hair and human babies drink their mother's milk. It contains all the goodness that a growing human baby needs.

Primates

Humans are primates. This is a subgroup of mammals that includes lemurs and lorises on the one hand and tarsiers, monkeys and apes (including humans) on the other.

Haplorhines

Humans are haplorhines, meaning 'simple noses', a group which includes monkeys and apes. One difference between monkeys and apes is very obvious: most monkeys have tails but apes do not, which, if you look in the mirror, makes us an ape.

What's in a name?

The scientific species name for modern humans is *Homo sapiens*, meaning 'wise human being'. In biology, most living things have a two-word name. In this case, *Homo*, meaning 'human', is the genus name, and *sapiens*, meaning 'wise', is the specific name. In the following pages, you will find the two-word names of several of our ancestors, although some will just have the genus name so the words are less of a mouthful.

SMALL BEGINNINGS

The earliest primate fossils are about 65 million years old, and those animals evolved from primate-like creatures that were living when dinosaurs ruled the Earth. They were small and kept out of the way of dinosaurs by living in trees.

Asteroid impact!

About 66 million years ago, an asteroid hit the Earth and three-quarters of the world's wildlife became extinct, including the dinosaurs. It also meant that a quarter of life survived. Among the survivors were the early primates. With many of their competitors and predators gone, new species of primates evolved, and one of them was our direct ancestor.

Small bodies, big brains

Our earliest primate ancestors resembled modern tree shrews, tiny rodent-like mammals that scamper around in the tropical forest. Tree shrews have relatively large brain sizes for their bodies, so the early primates were probably pretty smart for their size.

PURGATORIUS

Pronounced: Perg-a-tor-ee-us
Lived: Cretaceous period – Paleocene epoch (66 mya)
Size: rat-sized, 15 cm long

This potential early primate survived the mass extinction and went on to live in the trees. It had ankle bones that could rotate and adjust the position of its feet, allowing it to grab branches easily. It was probably not a direct ancestor of humans, but our ancient relative would have looked and behaved like it.

Eyes front!

Like *Purgatorius* and modern tree shrews, our ancestors probably had eyes on the sides of their heads. These were good for spotting approaching predators. Later primates had eyes on the front of the head, like we have, providing the animals with a better way to judge distances. It gave them an advantage in finding food in the trees, and was especially useful for catching fast-moving insects.

ARCHICEBUS

Pronounced: Arch-ee-see-bus
Lived: Eocene epoch (55 mya)
Size: body 9 cm

Archicebus was tiny. It was smaller than the smallest living primate – Berthe's mouse lemur. Its eyes looked forwards. It possessed a long monkey-like tail, grasping hands, and its toes ended in flat nails, like we have, rather than claws. Scientists think it is probably not a direct ancestor to humans, but it looked a lot like one.

Vitamin deficiency

The primates that gave rise to humans lost a very important function. They could not make vitamin C, which means that we, as their descendents, can't either. It is something we share with modern guinea pigs, monkeys and other apes. The answer was to eat fruits, which are rich in vitamin C. It was our quest for fruit that, as you will see, helped shape the course of early human evolution.

AGE OF THE APES

Most of the earliest primate fossils have been found in Europe and Asia, but fossils from 30 million years ago show that, in Africa, monkey-like ape ancestors were beginning to look more like the apes we know today. Our distant ancestors were starting to look a little more like us, although they still lived in the trees where a key part of their diet was fruit.

Evolving together

Not all animals see in colour like we do, and that ability may have had something to do with fruit. Scientists have suggested that primates and fruit trees may have evolved together. The trees produced fruit that was increasingly more colourful and attractive as it ripened. Primates evolved the ability to see it in colour, reach for it, and pick it at the right time. Primates ate the fruit and dispersed the seeds in their droppings. The tree depended on primates and primates depended on the tree.

AEGYPTOPITHECUS

Pronounced: Ee-jip-tow-pith-uh-cus
Lived: Oligocene (30 mya)
Size: same as a modern howler monkey

This primate had features of both Old World monkeys and apes. It had a monkey's tail, but an ape's arm bones. It lived in large troops in the swamp forests of northeast Africa. Males had large, pointed canine teeth, so it is likely they fought to become the boss, like modern baboons.

PROCONSUL

Pronounced: Proh-con-sul
Lived: Miocene epoch (25-23 mya)
Size: same as a chimpanzee

Proconsul was a primate that looked more like an ape than a monkey. It had no tail, an ape-like face, and it could grasp things better than a monkey. It also had a few leftover monkey features, such as a long, flexible back, and it probably walked on all fours on the topside of branches like monkeys do.

PIEROLAPITHECUS

Pronounced: Peer-ow-la-pith-uh-cus
Lived: Miocene epoch (13 to 12.5 mya)
Size: 1 m tall

Pierolapithecus was a tree-dwelling ape. It had an ape's rigid lower back, so it sat with its body in an upright position, like a chimpanzee. Its kneecap was shaped like a modern ape's, which gave it good knee movement, and it had flexible wrists. These features show it was good at climbing upwards and downwards, meaning it probably came down from the trees and travelled on the ground. It had wide hips, which gave it greater balance than a monkey. It might have walked on all fours using its knuckles, like a gorilla, or even stood upright to look for danger. It was, or was similar to, the last common ancestor of gorillas, chimpanzees and humans.

HOW DO WE KNOW WHO OUR ANCESTORS WERE?

As pre-human primates lived many millions of years ago, their fossils are the main reason scientists know they existed. Fossils are the parts of plants and animals that have been preserved. They can be made in many ways. One way is to be buried in sediments, such as those on a lake bed. Over time, minerals replace the tissues, so fossils become like stone. Hard parts, such as bone, make for better fossils than soft parts, like brains. Tracks and burrows can also fossilise. They are known as 'trace fossils'. One way scientists know how old fossils are is by working out the age of the rocks in which they were found.

Brain size

In human evolution, the size of the brain is one indication of how smart its owner might have been. But, if brains don't fossilise, how do we know how big they were? The brain usually fits tightly into the space inside the skull so, using X-rays and CT scans, scientists can measure the size of the inside of a fossil skull. The size of the cavity gives an idea of the size of the brain.

Looking back with DNA

Genes are made of sequences of DNA, the chemical blueprint in the nucleus of all our cells. It not only gives each of us a unique identity, but also shows how we are related. By tracking back these genetic relationships between animals, scientists can work out who an animal's ancestors were, who was closely or distantly related, and even where and when they lived.

MEET THE RELATIVES

As all living things evolved from the same common ancestor, we share genes with every living thing on Earth, some more than others. We share 99.9% of genes with other modern humans, 96% with chimpanzees, 90% with cats, 85% with mice and about 60% with insects. You differ genetically by only 4% from chimpanzees and bonobos, making them your closest non-human relatives alive today.

Who was there?

Finding miniscule traces of DNA is helping scientists to determine what plants and animals were present in the places that feature in the human story. In a cave in Belgium, for example, there were no fossil skull fragments or other parts of a skeleton present, yet scientists were able to find minute amounts of DNA in the sediment of the cave floor — probably from blood, wee or poo — revealing that ancient humans had once lived there.

WALKING UPRIGHT

At some point between 8 and 6 million years ago, our nearest living relatives, the chimpanzees and bonobos, split away from our branch of the tree of life. It was a big moment in human history, for we were now hominins and on the branch that would lead directly to modern humans... but there were a few stages to go through first, such as walking upright.

Hips and knees

Chimpanzees and gorillas can walk upright, but they do so with bent legs. The joints at the top of the thigh bone and knee are such that they cannot stand straight on one leg, so they have to swing their body over when they raise their leg to walk, which makes them wobble from side to side. Nevertheless, they can walk upright and climb about in the trees. They bridge two worlds.

Why walk upright?

We don't know for sure, but it is generally said that our early ancestors stood up on two legs when they moved out of the forest and onto the grassy savannahs. This way, they could see further across the plains. All the early hominins, however, spent a good part of their lives in the trees, so there must be other reasons. One suggestion is that it has something to do with holding and carrying. By standing up, hominins had their hands free to hold tools, and carry food and even babies.

Other benefits

Early humans might have stood on their hind legs to appear bigger and more ferocious, like bears do. Walking and running also enabled early humans to cover open ground more easily, so they could search a wider area for sources of food, and on the hot savannah standing up exposes less of the body to the sun.

'ARDI' THE WALKER

'Ardi' is the nickname of *Ardipithecus*, a primitive ape that showed ape-like and hominin-like features. The first Ardi fossils were of a female who was very much like a chimpanzee in size and stature. It indicates that our direct ancestor, who lived at about the same time, was also chimp-sized. Ardi had a smallish brain, even smaller than a modern chimpanzee's. She lived in woodlands in what is now Ethiopia.

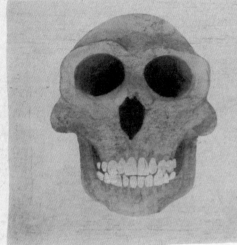

STAY AT HOME DAD

Ardi had small teeth like a human. Even male canine teeth – the pointy ones either side of the front teeth – were small. This tells us that there was little aggression between males in *Ardipithecus* society. Where male primates fight, canine teeth tend to be long and fang-like. Ardi's small teeth have led one scientist to suggest that the non-aggressive males actually helped with the rearing of children, a key behaviour in later human evolution.

THE CLUE IS IN THE BONES

Ardi had a grasping big toe on each foot, which would have been used to help her climb trees, but her pelvis bones show there was something even more important about her: Ardi could also be 'bipedal'. In other words, when she was on the ground, she could walk upright on her back legs, a bit like we do. By walking this way, she became one of the first hominins.

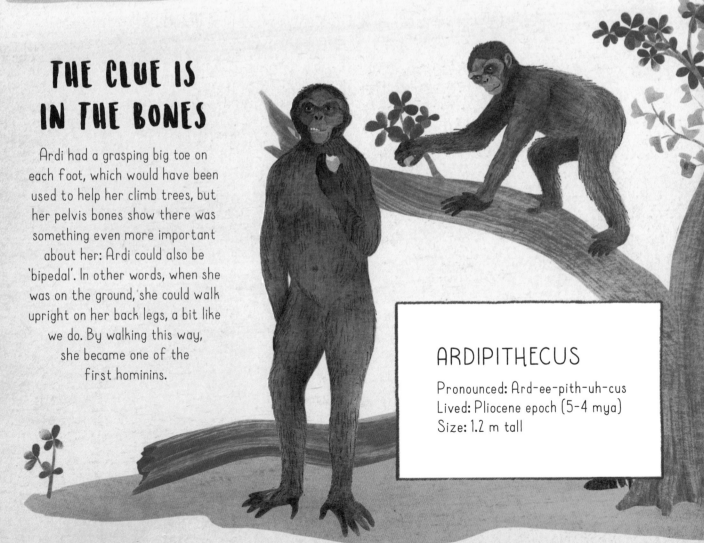

ARDIPITHECUS

Pronounced: Ard-ee-pith-uh-cus
Lived: Pliocene epoch (5-4 mya)
Size: 1.2 m tall

'LUCY' AND THE FIRST TOOLS

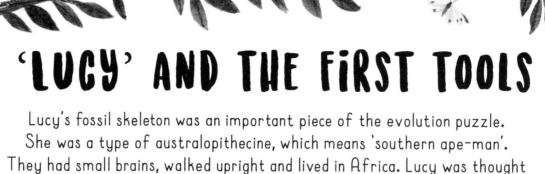

Lucy's fossil skeleton was an important piece of the evolution puzzle. She was a type of australopithecine, which means 'southern ape-man'. They had small brains, walked upright and lived in Africa. Lucy was thought to be 12–18 years old but was a mature adult. She lived in woodlands in what is now Ethiopia in eastern Africa over three million years ago. She could have been one of our ancestors.

Lucy in the sky

Lucy received her nickname because, at the time her discoverers were celebrating their find, they were playing The Beatles' recording *Lucy in the Sky with Diamonds*. At that time (before Ardi had been discovered), she was the earliest known of our human-like relatives.

Lucy's diet

Lucy's belly was big, like a chimpanzee's. This allowed space for a large stomach and the long intestines needed to process her food. Her species mostly ate leaves, grasses and fruit with probably some meat. She may even have used tools. An *Australopithecus* child who lived 3.3 million years ago was found with fossil animal bones that may have been broken to get at the marrow inside. Bones with scratch marks have also been discovered. They were probably made with simple stone tools, one of the earliest records of tool use by our hominin relatives.

AUSTRALOPITHECUS AFARENSIS

Pronounced: aw-stra-loh-*pith*-uh-cus ah-far-en-sis

Lived: Pliocene epoch (3.85 to 2.95 mya)

Size: male 1.5 m, female 1.1 m tall

What does Lucy's skeleton tell us?

Lucy had long arms with curved fingers for climbing, like a chimpanzee, but the bottom half of her body was more human-like. She had a short, bowl-shaped pelvis like we have. It supported her upper body and kept it upright. Her thigh bones were shaped like ours, so the weight of her body was over her strong knees. She had arched feet that supported each step. She walked more like a human than Ardi did, but she also spent a third of her life up in the trees. She may have slept up there, safe from predators.

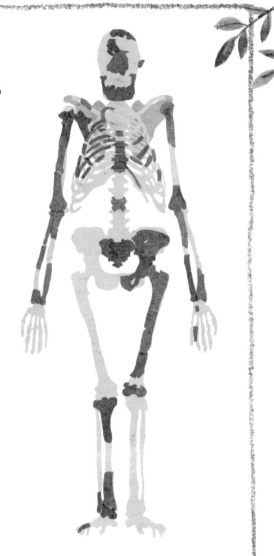

First team players

Lucy's species probably did not kill the animals being butchered. They most likely scavenged from carcasses killed by predators. It meant they competed with them for the same food, so some degree of teamwork must have been used to outwit and not fall prey to their rivals. Sharp stones, used to quickly cut away the meat, gave them an advantage.

TOOL MAKERS

Lucy and her kind were not the only hominins to use stone tools. Other early hominins were making them too. These early tool kits are called 'Oldowan', as the first stone tools to be discovered were found in Olduvai Gorge in Tanzania.

Oldowan tool kit

The Oldowan toolmaker used one stone, such as a river cobble, to bash against another, usually quartz, obsidian or flint, to produce sharp-edged flakes that could be used like knives. Obsidian flakes have a cutting edge far sharper than the finest steel blade. Even today, some surgeons use obsidian blades because they cause the least damage to tissues.

First tool production

Although the first tools to be discovered were in Tanzania, the world's earliest known stone tools were found later in neighbouring Kenya, about the same time that Lucy was living in Ethiopia. The toolkit includes sharp-edged flakes, round hammers and large anvils. Rocks must have been brought and struck against the anvil to make the thin, sharp flakes used to cut meat. Who made those Kenyan tools is unknown but *Australopithecus* like Lucy are key candidates.

Chimp tools

At one time, it was thought tool-use was unique to humans, but we now know that many animals use tools. Chimpanzees make rods to 'fish' for termites and sharp sticks to spear bushbabies, and use rock hammers and anvils to crack nuts. It is quite possible the common ancestor of humans and chimps was a tool-user more than 6 million years ago.

HANDY MAN

The first toolmaker to be discovered was *Homo habilis*, meaning 'handy man'. He was the first member of the genus *Homo* to be recognised. He is our own genus, but he was the least like modern humans. He lived in eastern and southern Africa, probably on the edge of woodlands, where he was an omnivore.

Handy man had a slightly larger brain than Lucy – just under half the size of a modern human brain – and a smaller face, but he still had long, ape-like arms. He walked upright on two legs, but also climbed trees.

HOMO HABILIS

Pronounced: Hoh-mo ha-bill-is
Lived: Pleistocene epoch (2.4 to 1.4 mya)
Size: male 1.35 m, female 1 m tall

Scavengers and predators

Like Lucy, *Homo habilis* was probably not a hunter. He scavenged carcasses, but he had to be careful. Several predators caught and ate early humans. They included leopards, an extinct species of hyena, and two species of extinct sabre-toothed cat: *Megantereon* and *Dinofelis*, both about the size of a modern jaguar.

Climate change

Homo habilis lived at a time when the climate was changing. It was cooler and drier, which led to fewer forests and more grassland. This meant there were fewer forest foods to be had, forcing forest dwellers to search for new sources of food. This challenge led to another spurt in early human evolution. Meat became an important part of their diet.

WE HAVE FIRE!

For thousands of years, our ancestors ate raw meat, huddled together in the cold, and slept in tree nests on the ground in the dark, fearful of marauding predators, but then all that changed: they discovered how to control fire.

Big appetite

Large bodies and big brains needed a lot of energy, and therefore food. Long legs meant that early hominins could cover a lot of ground during a day, and a larger brain meant that they could select the higher-quality foods, such as animal protein. They ate meat from carcasses that they both hunted and scavenged. They might have stolen food from the same big cats that could do them harm, such as *Dinofelis* (right).

Hunting and butchering

About 1.8 million years ago, early hominins made and used more complex tools, such as axes and cleavers, which were more sophisticated than anything chimpanzees and earlier hominins could make. They were called Acheulean tools. At the same time, the wrist was evolving, so those with strong wrists could handle the tools better than those with weak wrists. They had better chances of survival.

Fires and cooking

These hominins did not chew as much as our more ancient relatives because they cooked their food. The oldest possible evidence for this was found in a cave in South Africa, where it appears meat and bone had been cooked over a small campfire. It was about one million years old. The campfire would have kept our ancestors safe too. Many wild animals are afraid of fire.

Caring for the sick and elderly

A fossil skull, about 1.7 million years old, has been found that is almost toothless. The empty tooth sockets had been reabsorbed, which could only happen if the teeth were lost while the owner was still alive. It shows that hominin groups at this time must have cared for their old or ill members.

UPRIGHT HUMAN

The pioneering hominin who achieved so much was *Homo erectus*, meaning 'upright man'. He was bigger, smarter, faster and more human-like than any who had gone before.

HOMO ERECTUS

Pronounced: Hoh-mo ee-reck-tus
Lived: Pleistocene epoch (1.8 mya to 143,000 years ago)
Size: up to 1.85 m tall

Growing brains

The brain of *Homo erectus* was significantly bigger than the brains of earlier hominins. Early individuals had a brain that was about 60 per cent of the size of a modern human brain, but later ones had brains about the size of the smallest modern adult human brain. *Homo erectus* was smart.

World traveller

Homo erectus was a cosmopolitan hominin. His remains, about 1.8 million years old, have been found in East Africa and Georgia, but later he reached Spain to the northwest and China and Indonesia in the east, which meant that *Homo erectus* was adapted to survive in many different types of habitat, much like modern humans do today.

A body like ours

Early specimens of *Homo erectus* are the oldest known hominins with modern human body proportions. Body size ranged from short to tall, as in modern human populations, but they all had long legs and short arms. *Homo erectus* had abandoned the trees and was a dedicated walker and runner.

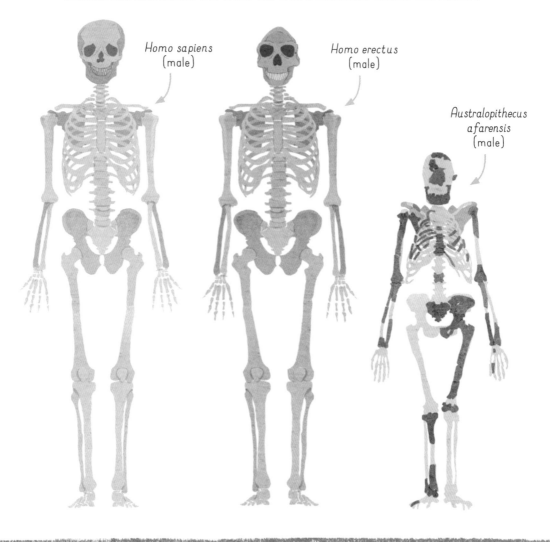

Homo sapiens
(male)

Homo erectus
(male)

Australopithecus afarensis
(male)

First sailors

To reach islands in Indonesia, *Homo erectus* would have had to cross the sea. We don't know how *Homo erectus* reached islands such as Flores in Indonesia where they were living by 800,000 years ago. They could have been washed across bodies of water on mats of vegetation during tsunamis, but some scientists believe they could have built rafts and actively paddled.

First words

Some scientists believe that *Homo erectus* developed speech. He would not have been able to utter the same range of sounds as modern humans, but with just a few sounds he could have the makings of a simple language. Handing on the knowledge and skills to make complex tools might have led to communication in more than grunts and gestures.

SOMEWHERE TO LIVE

Early hominins lived mainly in hot places, such as Africa and southern Asia, but some of them moved north into Europe. A few even reached Britain. They were looking for new sources of food. The new lands had plenty of food sources, including deer, bison and rhinos, so they stayed. The winters were sometimes cold, but this led to new advances, such as building shelters and wearing simple clothes.

There's no place like home

Shelters helped protect their owners from the wind and rain. Hominins used caves as shelters, but the first shelters actually built were simple structures made from wood, rocks, and animal skins. What look like 400,000-year-old shelters have been discovered in France. Some scientists believe they were simple tents held up by poles and surrounded by stones, and some were up to 14 metres long. Inside were stone hearths and even windbreaks to protect the fire from the wind. A hole in the roof let the smoke from the fire escape.

Down by the river

Early hominins often set up camps on islands in the flood plains of rivers. Wild horses, deer and rhinos fed on the grasses growing there. Birds' eggs, eels and other fish, and water plants made for a balanced diet. The islands were also safe from predatory big cats, which tend to avoid water.

HEIDELBERG MAN

One species of hominin that made it from Africa to Europe was *Homo heidelbergensis*. This species had features that were similar to *Homo erectus*, *Homo neanderthalensis* and *Homo sapiens*. They included a large brain and flatter face, like a modern human, but with heavy brow ridges above the eyes and without a pointed chin, like *Homo erectus* and *Homo neanderthalensis*. *Homo heidelbergensis* was tall and strong, with powerful leg muscles for running quickly. The brain size was midway between *Homo erectus* and *Homo neanderthalensis* (see page 24).

HOMO HEIDELBERGENSIS

Pronounced: Ho-mo high-del-berg-en-sis
Lived: Pleistocene epoch (700,000 to 200,000 years ago)
Size: 1.57 to 1.75 m tall

Moving north

Fossils, possibly of *Homo heidelbergensis*, have been found in Africa, Asia and Europe. When their migration from Africa to Europe began, the climate was warm and the weather was fair. These conditions were ideal for spreading northwards. It was only later that the climate changed, turning colder. These hominins had to adapt to the changing conditions.

Wooden spears

Homo heidelbergensis had stone tools similar to Acheulean tools, but thinner and more carefully shaped. Wooden spears with stone tips were added to the tool kit, as well as scrapers made of deer antlers and bone. *Homo heidelbergensis* was one of the first hominins to regularly hunt large animals, some as big as elephants. They used spears to bring down prey and hand axes and stone flakes to cut away the meat and break open the bones to reach the marrow inside.

THE HUMAN PUZZLE

The position of *Homo heidelbergensis* in the human story is controversial. Some scientists believe Heidelberg man was the last common ancestor of modern humans and the Neanderthals. African populations gave rise to modern humans and European populations to Neanderthals. Others think that the only fossil bones that should be included as *Homo heidelbergensis* are European and they are the ancestors of Neanderthals. Still others argue that *Homo heidelbergensis* was not a single species at all, but that the fossils are from several species that evolved at the same time. The human story is so complex that nobody is sure who is right.

NEANDERTHALS

At some time between 430,000 and 250,000 years ago, an advanced type of hominin evolved. It was not our direct ancestor, but it was our closest extinct relative – *Homo neanderthalensis*, also known as the Neanderthal. Neanderthals lived in Europe and southwest Asia at about the same time modern humans were evolving in Africa.

What did they look like?

Neanderthals were stockier and stronger than modern humans, with bigger bodies, shorter legs, and muscular arms. They had wide noses and large brow ridges above the eyes. The eyes themselves were big, as was the part of their brain that dealt with vision. The brains of Neanderthals were slightly bigger on average than ours.

HOMO NEANDERTHALENSIS

Pronounced: Ho-mo nee-ander-tal-en-sis
Lived: Pleistocene epoch (430,000 to 38,000 years ago)
Size: male 1.68 m, female 1.55 m tall

Precision tools

Neanderthals manufactured cutting flakes and hand axes. They often pre-shaped stone cores into half-finished tools that could be given a sharp cutting edge later. This technique meant they could travel away from the place where they quarried the rocks. While out hunting, they could make tools when they were needed.

Neanderthal nosh

In Africa, plant food was available all year round, but during a northern European winter Neanderthals had fewer plants to eat. Instead, they ate much more meat – reindeer in winter and red deer in summer, for example, along with aurochs, mammoths, straight-tusked elephants and woolly rhino. Neanderthals living near the coast in Gibraltar hunted or scavenged seals and dolphins, caught fish, and collected mussels. The meat was probably cooked over fires. Neanderthals also ate plants and mushrooms when they were available. One group in northwest Spain ate forest mosses, pine nuts and mushrooms.

JUST LIKE US?

In many respects, Neanderthals behaved like humans. However, as more Neanderthal material is unearthed, the differences in behaviour between humans and Neanderthals are becoming less. Nevertheless, if one were on a crowded street today, it would probably stand out from the crowd.

Clothes and jewellery

The Neanderthals probably wore clothes. Their tool kit included scrapers to clean animal hides. These hides were probably worn as blankets or poncho-like garments. Possible jewellery made from eagle talons, along with pierced animal teeth and carved ivory have been found at Neanderthal sites, some of it 130,000 years old.

Cave homes

Neanderthals also spent time creating homes. A cave shelter in Italy that was divided into three areas shows how organized they were. The top level was for butchering game, the middle level for sleeping, and the lower level at the cave entrance was where tools were made. We now know that Neanderthals even decorated their caves. Red ladder shapes, hand stencils, and red lines and dots have been found in Spanish caves, dating back at least 64,000 years, before prehistoric humans arrived. There are also geometric scratch marks made by Neanderthals on a cave wall in Gibraltar.

Mysterious Denisovans

The Denisovans were mysterious hominins, closely related to Neanderthals, who once lived across Asia, from Siberia to Southeast Asia. We only know they existed because DNA has been found that is neither Neanderthal nor human. Many Melanesians, Aboriginal Australians, and Papuans today have a little Denisovan DNA.

The end of the Neanderthals

After a very cold period, the Neanderthals were forced to the southern edges of Europe. At the same time, modern humans were spreading across Europe. When the temperature rose again, the Neanderthals were probably prevented from returning to their old lands by the new invaders. Very few survived, and by 40,000 years ago the species was extinct. However, DNA analysis shows that Neanderthals interbred with modern humans about 50,000 years ago. It means that, even today, some of us have some Neanderthal DNA.

MODERN HUMANS

We used to think that *Homo sapiens* evolved in Eastern Africa, but fossils of a similar age showing characteristics of our species have now been found in Morocco, Ethiopia and South Africa. This makes the picture of our origins more complicated and suggests more *Homo sapiens*-like groups might have been evolving right across the continent. We evolved at a time when the climate changed back and forth. Cold and dry periods were separated by warm and wet phases. It meant that humans either had to find ways to survive these extremes, or migrate to other areas. These changes shaped the lives of humans, and we used our highly developed brains to meet the challenge.

HOMO SAPIENS

Pronounced: Ho-mo sap-ee-ens
Lived: 300,000 to the present
Size: average European 1.75 m tall

Meet the humans

Homo sapiens is lightly built, with a domed brain case, flat face, jutting chin and forehead without heavy brow ridges. Brain size matches body size, so lightweight prehistoric humans had a brain capacity of 1500 cubic centimetres, and the even lighter modern human has a brain size of 1350 cubic centimetres. The bulky Neanderthal had a correspondingly bigger brain, about 1700 cubic centimetres.

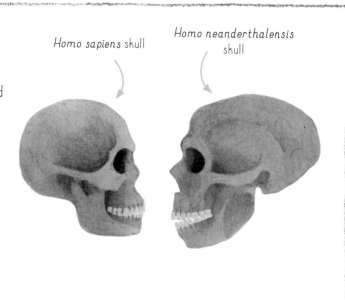

Homo sapiens skull

Homo neanderthalensis skull

The muddle in the middle

It was once thought that there was a single evolutionary line from *Homo habilis* to *Homo erectus* and then to *Homo sapiens*. Scientists now believe our story unfolded in a much more complex way. There were many different types of early humans scattered across Africa, separated by rivers, mountains, deserts and other geographical barriers. Each population evolved at its own pace and in its own way, though we know that they did interbreed. Eventually – and nobody knows precisely how, where and why – *Homo sapiens* evolved.

Great survivors

Humans are the last surviving hominins. All the rest are extinct. Some scientists believe that we thrived because we are 'generalist specialists'. This may sound like a contradiction, but it's not. Like any generalist animal, humans make use of a variety of resources and can live in a range of different environments. But we also have specialist populations, such as those that live high in the mountains, where the air is thin, and Arctic hunters, who can survive in very cold climates. So, as a species, we are generalists and specialists at the same time.

Arctic animals

In the past, Arctic peoples obtained everything they needed from the animals they hunted. Clothes and kayak coverings, for example, were made from sealskins.

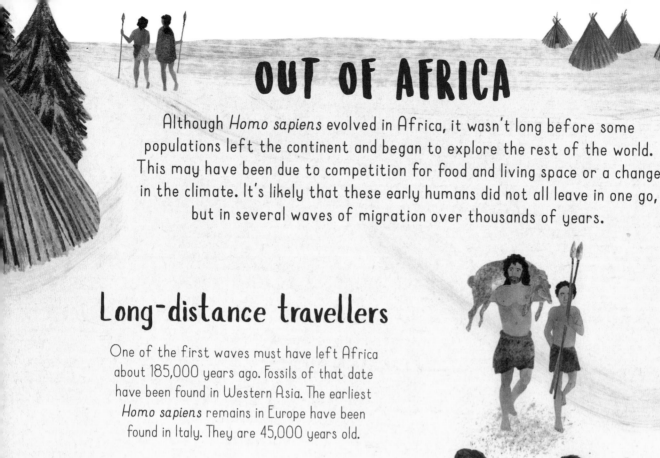

OUT OF AFRICA

Although *Homo sapiens* evolved in Africa, it wasn't long before some populations left the continent and began to explore the rest of the world. This may have been due to competition for food and living space or a change in the climate. It's likely that these early humans did not all leave in one go, but in several waves of migration over thousands of years.

Long-distance travellers

One of the first waves must have left Africa about 185,000 years ago. Fossils of that date have been found in Western Asia. The earliest *Homo sapiens* remains in Europe have been found in Italy. They are 45,000 years old.

The first Australians

Another wave of humans took the so-called 'southern route' to avoid a cold spell. They followed the coasts of southern Asia. By 50,000 years ago, about 3,000 of them had crossed the sea to reach northern Australia. Stone axes with wooden handles and ancient campfires have been found there. These pioneers co-existed with giant wombats and wallabies, and a monster monitor lizard.

Coming to America

Humans had arrived in North America by 20,000 years ago, travelling from Siberia. Sea levels were lower than they are today, so they may have walked across a land bridge that joined Asia with the Americas. Another theory is that they followed the southern shore of the land bridge in boats.

MASS EXTINCTION OF MEGAFAUNA

In North America, migrants shared the continent with large animals, such as mastodons, sabre-toothed cats, short-faced bears and dire wolves – known as megafauna, meaning 'big animals'. They became extinct just after humans arrived. Did these people hunt the animals to extinction, or was there something else involved, such as a change in climate? Nobody is sure.

Human
Average height:
1.6-1.75 m

Short faced bear
Average height:
1.8 m

Mastodon
Average height:
2.45-3 m

Direwolf
Average height:
0.6 m

SMART HUNTERS

Our prehistoric ancestors were skilled hunters. An ability to run long distances enabled them to chase animals to exhaustion, but they also found inventive ways of finding, catching and killing their prey.

Prehistoric bowmen

The earliest known evidence for the bow and arrow was discovered in South Africa, at a site that dates back about 77,000 years. The bow is a much longer-range weapon than a spear, so hunters who used it didn't need to get close to their prey. They could hide behind bushes or rocks rather than be out in the open and give themselves away. They could also carry several arrows rather than a single spear.

First map?

About 27,000 years ago, a group of hunters in the Pavlov Hills of the Czech Republic scratched marks onto a mammoth tusk. The engravings may represent the hills and valleys around them. This would mean that they had a map, probably a hunting map that showed them where they were, where they could go, and where to find the animals they hunted.

Game drive

In western Asia archaeologists have found the remains of huge enclosures built of stones. These were traps, known as 'desert kites' due to their shape. Prehistoric human hunters understood the migratory routes taken by their target animals and drove them into the trap and killed them. These pens, which are up to 6,000 years old, were the first slaughterhouses – there is evidence of up to 100 Persian gazelles killed in a single drive.

Buffalo jumps

In North America, hunters herded wild bison and drove them over steep cliffs. The herds were guided between piles of rocks or 'driving lanes', which, like the desert kites, funnelled the animals to the cliff edge. The animals broke their legs, and hunters finished them off them with spears. The first buffalo jumps took place more than 12,000 years ago, and they continued right up until about 500 years ago.

MAKING LIFE EASIER

Humans are not the only species to use tools, but we are the only animals that make complex tools. It all started with simple stone tools like our hominin ancestors, but over the centuries more durable and flexible materials have been used – copper, tin, bronze, iron, steel, aluminium, and high-tech carbon fibre. Tools have enabled us to construct buildings from simple huts to space stations, and machines from simple levers and pulleys to the world's fastest supercomputer.

Harpoon

A whole new toolkit

Prehistoric *Homo sapiens* made and used stone tools, like their predecessors. However, the blades were more refined, such as long-bladed knives and long spearheads. Bone, ivory and antlers were added to the materials used. Fishhooks, barbed harpoons, bows and arrows, throwing spears, sickles, and sewing needles made of bone were added to the toolkit.

Fire control

Homo sapiens had a greater control of fire than earlier hominins. Round hearths and firepits enabled them to survive in colder parts of the world. Pottery kilns in the Czech Republic, about 26,000 years old, could fire ceramic figurines at temperatures over 400°C.

A sticky story

Some weapons consisted of sharp stone tools mounted on wooden handles and held in place using some sort of glue. In South Africa, scientists have worked out how they made the glue. They prepared a mixture of ochre, plant gums and fatty materials from animals, then used fire to get the mixture to the right consistency. This glue was about 65,000 years old.

Plant gums

Bone fragments

Ochre

Inventing the wheel

The wheel is a hugely important invention that has changed the course of history. The first wheel was a heavy stone potter's wheel, which was turned by hand. It was in use more than 6000 years ago in Western Asia. Not long afterwards, carts with solid wooden wheels appeared, but nobody is sure who invented them. The first picture of one is on a 5500-year-old clay pot discovered in Poland.

TIME TO EAT!

Prehistoric humans collected plants and hunted or scavenged animals. By 164,000 years ago they were harvesting and cooking shellfish and by 90,000 years ago they had tools to catch fish. They were also trying out new foods and by about 15,000 years ago even baking bread, although they wouldn't grow their own crops for thousands of years.

Starchy surprise

In a cave in Mozambique, scientists have uncovered stone tools that had starch residues, allowing them to work out what the prehistoric hunter-gatherers were eating. Wild foods included false banana roots, pigeon peas, and the African potato, but there was also sorghum, a wild grass seed that is still cultivated in Africa today. The big surprise was that the site is 100,000 years old. The discovery shows that prehistoric humans were eating grains long before farming began.

The seeds of agriculture

In Israel, scientists found remains of several simple brush huts. One of the huts contained burned seeds and fruits, including almonds, grapes and olives. These were wild versions of foods that would later become important crops. These early humans, who lived about 23,000 years ago, may have been trying out new foods to increase their food supply – a step towards farming and permanent settlements.

Wild porridge

A 32,000-year-old tool for grinding grain has been found in Italy. It was used to grind wild oats. The grains were dried by fire before grinding, providing evidence of prehistoric humans using different processes to prepare food. The grinder was used years before the dawn of agriculture.

Prehistoric toast

The remains of the oldest known bread are toasted crumbs found in Jordan. They are 14,400 years old. Bread was probably made because it was compact, portable, and provided carbohydrates and essential vitamins. It was baked on large circular stone fireplaces. Breadmaking was probably one of the reasons humans eventually began growing cereal crops.

HOW TO MAKE PREHISTORIC BREAD

Have a go at making your own prehistoric bread! Try different amounts of the ingredients, as prehistoric humans must have done, until you have bread that tastes good.

1. Mix wheat and barley flour.

2. Add ground chick peas and lentils.

3. Mix with water to make a dough.

4. With an adult's help, cook on a hob or in an oven.

PUTTING DOWN ROOTS

At the end of the most recent ice age, about 12,000 years ago, the climate became warmer and wetter. About this time groups of humans began to settle down and live in one place. They dug the soil and scattered wild seeds so that they could produce their own food, rather than always having to hunt or collect it. It was backbreaking work, but these people were the first farmers.

The Fertile Crescent

Farming began in an area known as the 'Fertile Crescent', which stretches between Iran and the Nile Valley in Egypt. Farmers in this region began to alter nature by recognising which plants were most useful to them as food and using their seeds to cultivate more. Migration allowed the practice to spread to other parts of the world.

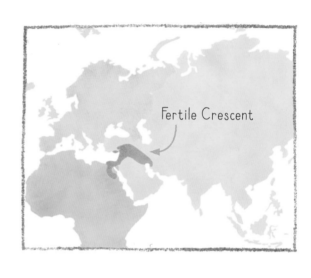

Fertile Crescent

Rice

Rice was one of the first grasses to be cultivated. All modern Asian rice varieties can trace their origin back to the Pearl River Valley in China about 13,500 years ago. Other varieties appeared elsewhere. Farmers grew rice in the Amazon Basin of Brazil about 4,000 years ago and the Niger River Delta in West Africa about 3,500 years ago.

American imports

Potatoes are native to the Americas. Almost every modern variety of potato can be traced back to potatoes grown on the islands of the Chiloé Archipelago, off the coast of Chile. There is a legend that Christopher Columbus was the first to bring them to Europe, with Sir Walter Raleigh introducing them to England. The truth is that Spanish conquistadors took them first to the Canary Islands, and then to the European mainland. Maize was first cultivated in southern Mexico about 9,000 years ago. Over the years, farmers selected plants that gave them more and more kernels until they created the kind of cobs that we see today.

Wheat
Location:
Southeast Turkey
Cultivation date:
10,000 years ago

Barley
Location:
Egypt,
Ethiopia, or Tibet
Cultivation date:
10,000 years ago

Rice
Location:
China
Cultivation date:
13,500 years ago

Maize
Location:
Mexico
Cultivation date:
10,000 years ago

Oats
Location:
Turkey or southeast Europe
Cultivation date:
3,000 years ago

SPICED UP

Our prehistoric ancestors liked their foods to be tasty. The residues of garlic, mustard and cooked onions have been found in the burned remains of food in pots about 6,100 years old. The spices that were used had little nutritional value, so their purpose must have been to add flavour to the food.

RUNNING WITH WOLVES

Taming and controlling nature wasn't just about plants — it extended to animals too. Through farming and herding, humans were starting to change nature. More food resulted in more people, so the human population increased dramatically. It was a turning point in the story of humans and of all life on Earth.

Wild and tame

Our ancestors domesticated four main categories of animals. The first were those that came to live alongside humans, such as dogs and cats. They also domesticated animals that were used for food, including cattle, sheep, goats, pigs, reindeer and alpacas. Horses, donkeys, camels and other pack animals were useful for pulling things or being ridden. Humans also domesticated a few types of insects, such as honey bees and silkworms.

Our best friend

Wolves were probably the first living things humans domesticated, even before any other plant or animal. The tamest wolves may have even domesticated themselves, approaching ancient human campsites to feed on leftover food. Eventually, they joined human hunters and the bond between human and wolf was established. Those wolves evolved into dogs when they came into contact with European hunter-gatherers at some time between 32,100 and 8,800 years ago. They were then bred for their most useful features: sheepdogs for herding, huskies for pulling sleds, greyhounds for hunting in deserts and grasslands, short-legged dogs for hunting in tight spaces, and mastiffs for guarding.

Sheep

Sheep were one of the first animals domesticated for their meat, as well as their milk, hides and wool. They were tamed in the Fertile Crescent more than 10,500 years ago. The ancestor of modern sheep, the mouflon, was a very adaptable wild sheep. It was able to survive in all kinds of habitats but overhunting nearly led to its demise. People captured some and kept them on farms. Domestication was one way they ensured they had enough mouflon meat to eat.

Cattle breeding

The origins of European cattle can be traced back to just 80 animals that lived in Iran about 10,500 years ago. A brave farmer tamed the aggressive wild aurochs. All the European farm cattle we see today originally came from that population. Cattle were also domesticated in the Indus Valley and maybe in Egypt.

SAY CHEESE

Once animals were farmed, our ancestors not only had high quality meat to hand, but also milk. Milk was processed to make butter and cheese. A cheese strainer about 7500 years old has been found in Poland.

VILLAGES, TOWNS AND CITIES

Agriculture changed the way many people lived. The hunter-gatherers abandoned their nomadic lifestyle and began to build simple settlements, usually beside lakes or rivers. These were followed by more structured villages, towns and cities.

Farming settlement

In northwest Jordan, Western Asia, a 10,300-year-old settlement called Ain Ghazal stands beside the Zarqa River. It was one of the first farming villages, and its people lived in rectangular stone and mud-brick houses. These farmers grew crops and herded sheep and goats on nearby mountains. They also hunted wild animals. Over 600 years, the settlement grew from a village to a small town, eventually housing 1600 people.

City life

The first cities were founded in the Fertile Crescent about 6500 years ago. One of the oldest known is Uruk in Iraq. Farming enabled them to store extra food and trade with other cities. Living in a city also meant that people could easily exchange ideas and share goods. On the downside, many people together helped spread diseases, and one city might try to raid another to steal its food and enslave its citizens – giving rise to the first wars. By about 5000 years ago, walled cities were common. These strongholds could protect their citizens from marauding armies.

Butcher, baker, candlestick maker

With cities came the need for specialist jobs. While the farmers were out tending their crops and herds, there was a need for somebody to bake the bread, sell the meat, and trade any extra with other cities. At least four types of workers emerged – farmer, baker, butcher, and merchant. As cities grew, more and more specialized jobs were created, such as architects, builders, engineers, doctors and lawyers.

BUYING AND SELLING

We know that by 130,000 years ago, prehistoric humans were already trading goods over distances of 300 kilometres. This type of exchange was a safety net. If conditions changed locally, and materials for tools or food were scarce, then people could rely on neighbours to help out. They made friends, exchanged gifts, and bartered food and other valuable resources in order to survive.

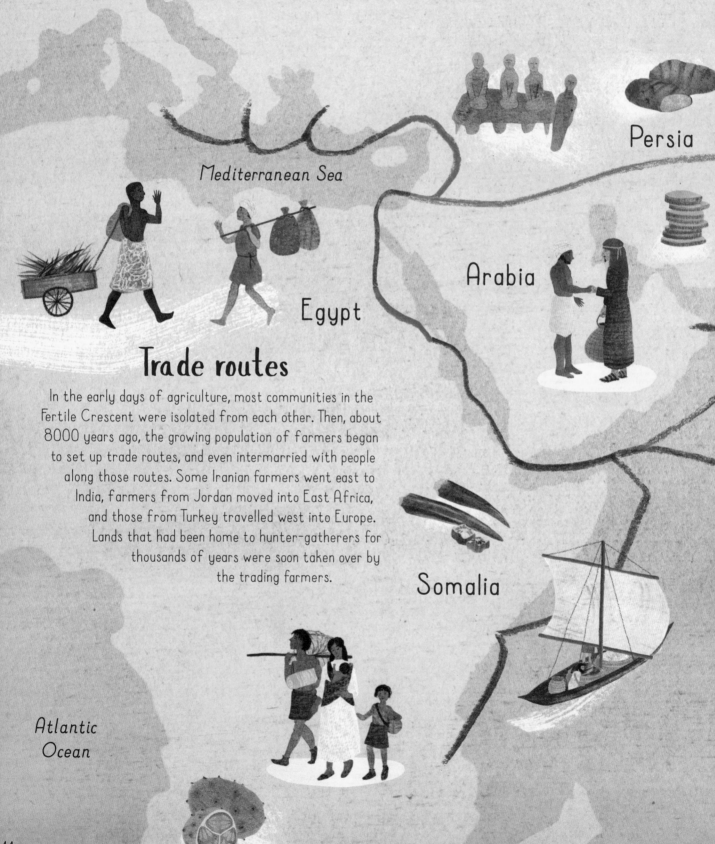

Persia

Mediterranean Sea

Arabia

Egypt

Trade routes

In the early days of agriculture, most communities in the Fertile Crescent were isolated from each other. Then, about 8000 years ago, the growing population of farmers began to set up trade routes, and even intermarried with people along those routes. Some Iranian farmers went east to India, farmers from Jordan moved into East Africa, and those from Turkey travelled west into Europe. Lands that had been home to hunter-gatherers for thousands of years were soon taken over by the trading farmers.

Somalia

Atlantic Ocean

The Silk Road

One of the longest ancient trading routes was known as the Silk Road, which connected Europe and eastern Asia. It was not a single road, but rather a network of routes over land and sea. It got its name from the silk that was exported from China, but all kinds of goods were carried. Traders first travelled the Silk Road about 1900 years ago, but in the 1300s it carried something nobody wanted – the Black Death, a plague that killed about half of Europe's population.

■ Sea route   ■ Land route

India

China

Indian Ocean

Seashell money

Before we had coins and banknotes, goods were sometimes paid for with seashells. There was one type of shell valued above all others – the money cowrie. It made a good currency because it was durable and impossible to forge. It is the shell of a sea creature that lives in the Indian and Pacific oceans. By 3000 years ago it had become the most common method of payment in Asia, Africa, Oceania and parts of Europe. It was in use as late as the 20th century.

HEALTH CARE

Without doctors, prehistoric humans with illnesses or injuries had a tough time. However, some of the fossil evidence shows that they may have tried to look after each other.

Time to heal

One skeleton found at Cro-Magnon in France had bones fused at the top of the backbone, indicating a bad back injury at some point in the past. Another had survived for some time with a fractured skull. The fact that they survived long enough for these injuries to heal shows that they might have received care from others in their group.

Apothecary apes

Prehistoric humans and even Neanderthals probably collected herbs and other plants that had medicinal properties to treat illnesses and injuries. We can guess this because our nearest living relatives, the chimpanzees, use herbal medicines. The leaves of a plant in the daisy family, for example, are good for getting rid of gut parasites. Chimps have been seen to fold the leaves and swallow them like we take a pill.

Early surgery

Skulls dating back 10,000 years have been found with very precise holes drilled or chiselled into them. Scientists believe this could have been an attempt to ease headaches. The hole in the top of the head was supposed to let 'badness' escape, and evidence of healing suggests some of these patients lived for a long time afterwards. It is similar to the way modern surgeons sometimes remove part of the skull to relieve pressure on the brain.

Antibiotics

The use of antibiotics may seem like a modern technique, but our ancestors came upon them by accident. Ancient Egyptians, for example, put mouldy bread on infected wounds. It wasn't until 1928, however, that Alexander Fleming discovered penicillin and proved that an antibiotic based on mould could stop the growth of bacteria.

Vaccines

Vaccination against diseases is also not as new as you might think. The ancient Greeks noticed that people who recovered from a disease called smallpox would not catch it again. By about 1,000 years ago, physicians had created a form of vaccination that involved putting smallpox scabs under the skin of healthy people, or grinding them into a powder that could be inhaled through the nose. This would stimulate the body to produce antibodies against the disease. It didn't always work, and people died instead of being protected. Edward Jenner began to successfully vaccinate people against smallpox in 1796.

JEWELLERY, TRINKETS AND CHARMS

The jewellery and other personal decorations that prehistoric humans and Neanderthals wore sent a silent message to other people. The jewellery might have been a way to identify a person's tribe or family, their status, or serve as a protection against evil spirits. Then again, they might have just looked nice and made the wearer feel good! This shows that prehistoric humans had moved on from simple survival and were now not only aware of themselves, but also concerned with their appearance.

Shell necklaces

Some of the earliest forms of jewellery have been discovered in Africa and Western Asia. They were sea snail shells that were pierced to make beads that could be strung and worn, possibly as a necklace. Some of the shells have red ochre inside. The date of the finds indicates that our ancestors were wearing jewellery over 100,000 years ago.

Prehistoric fashion

The first clothes were made from animal skins and furs. Those that were sewn together gave better protection against the elements than those that were simply tied. Fibres of flax plants, which had been dyed, are a clue that people were weaving clothes and baskets as early as 28,000 years ago. Some clothes were decorated with buttons and beads, and their owner might wear a carved pendant around their neck. A horse pendant found in Germany, carved from mammoth ivory, is 32,000 years old.

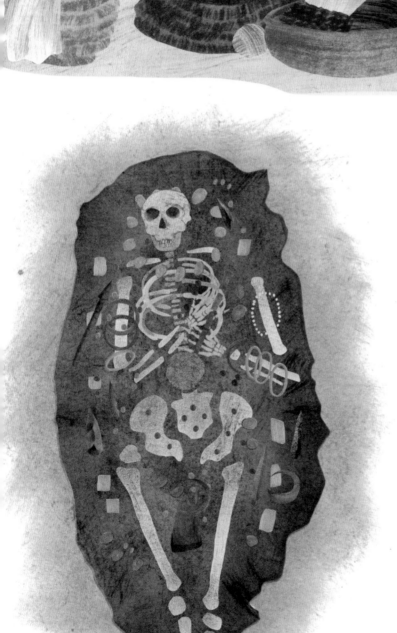

Precious gold

Humans have valued gold for thousands of years. It was probably first picked as nuggets from riverbeds and pieces have been found in caves. Gold might have been considered a symbol of power because it does not corrode. The oldest known manmade gold objects, including jewellery, are from Varna in Bulgaria. They are about 6,000 years old.

Jewellery makers

It was often assumed men made jewellery, while women cooked and looked after babies, but in Austria, scientists have discovered the grave of a female jewellery maker. Alongside the skeleton they found an anvil, hammers and flint chisels, and items of dress jewellery about 4000 years old. It was normal for a person's working tools to be buried with them, but this discovery was unusual. It means scientists need to look at prehistoric gender roles in a fresh light.

MAKING A MARK

Imagine how prehistoric humans might have looked at the world. For most of their lives, they focused on practical things – how to feed the family and find water, how to survive attacks by predators or their neighbours. However, when the practical tasks were completed, their creative skills were directed at something that was not necessarily useful but had beauty and triggered the emotions. Humans had discovered art.

Abstract art

The first potential works of art were very simple. Scientists have found a freshwater clamshell with a zigzag mark scratched onto it by *Homo erectus* about 500,000 years ago, perhaps using a shark's tooth.

Another early piece of abstract design comes from the Blombos Cave in South Africa. It is a dark red rectangular piece of ochre with a crosshatched engraving on the surface, made by early *Homo sapiens* about 73,000 years ago.

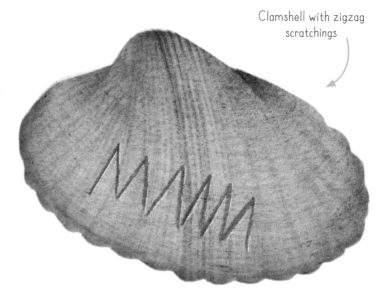
Clamshell with zigzag scratchings

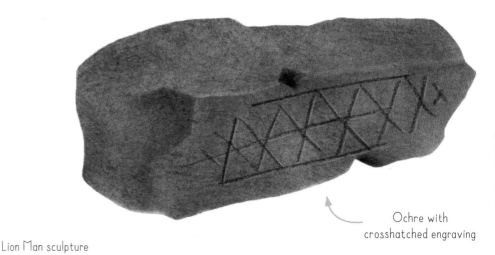
Ochre with crosshatched engraving

Lion Man sculpture

Half human, half lion

One of the world's oldest sculptures of a recognisable figure is the 'Lion Man', a creature with a human body and a lion's head. Found in Germany, it is carved from ivory and is 40,000 years old. Similar figures in neighbouring caves, along with simple bone flutes, suggest the figure may have been linked to some kind of religious cult.

Cave art

It is not fully understood why humans painted on the walls and ceilings of caves. The earliest art is of hand stencils and geometric shapes, but later images include the animals people encountered. This art may have had a purpose. It might have been part of a ritual: a way to bring luck during the hunt, or to make rain, or to keep the family safe from predators. The prehistoric artists went into deep and dark caves, so scientists believe the reason for their paintings were not just because they looked pretty. The materials used are mainly red, yellow and black pigments. The source of one pigment was 250 kilometres away, so the artist might have traded to obtain it.

GOOD FOR THE SOUL

Many people today turn to religion to help them through the ups and downs of everyday life, and it seems our prehistoric ancestors did something similar. Prehistoric humans relied on many aspects of the natural world for their very survival, so it comes as no surprise that they held such things as the Sun, wind, spectacular rocks and cave bears in high esteem, as well as their own ancestors. They might also have had concerns about good and bad spirits, which they might have soothed with offerings of food and sacrifices.

Formal burial

Losing loved ones must have been as difficult 100,000 years ago as it is today. The way prehistoric humans dealt with it back then was similar to the way we do now. The body was laid in a hole in the ground and covered. The person's worldly goods, such as stone tools, were buried with them. When humans settled in villages about 12,000 years ago, there are signs at one site at least that bodies were laid on beds of flowers and placed in cemeteries. Neanderthals may have buried their dead as well. A 50,000-year-old Neanderthal skeleton, discovered in France, looked as if it was folded into a grave.

ANIMAL WORSHIP

Signs of animal worship were discovered on Akab, an island near Dubai. About 6500 years ago it was a fishing village, where fishermen caught fish using hooks cut from oyster shells. At the site, scientists discovered a collection of dugong bones. They thought at first it was a butchery site, but closer inspection revealed the pile to be carefully constructed, with hints of red ochre. It was probably a sacred place, a monument to the dugongs that they hunted.

Mega-monument

The most famous prehistoric site in Europe is Stonehenge in England, the building of which began about 5,000 years ago. Here a circle of enormous 'sarsen' stones were hauled 30 km from the Marlborough Downs, with the bluestones or 'ringing rocks' coming from Wales, 320 km away. The stones are lined up with sunset at the winter solstice and sunrise at the summer solstice. Its function is unknown, but there are several theories. The graves found nearby suggest it could have been a burial site, but the number of deformed skeletons indicates it might have also been a healing site. It may also have been a place to celebrate ancestors, as well as an astronomical observatory to predict solstices, equinoxes and eclipses. Stonehenge was part of a huge complex with other henges and processional ways marked by stones.

LOOK WHO'S TALKING

Speech is a means of communication using words that represent objects, actions, feelings and ideas. These words consist of different combinations of sounds. When placed together in a particular order, they make a spoken language. Humans are the only living animals that truly speak, although a few birds can mimic us. However, it is thought Neanderthals and earlier hominins might have had simple spoken languages too.

Ancient voices

Using 3-D X-ray technology, scientists have been able to reveal that Neanderthals had similar body parts to produce speech as humans. If they had it, they probably used it. DNA research has shown that Neanderthals also had the same version of a special gene as humans – FOXP2 – which is essential for the development of speech and language.

Language origins

How speech began is one of the most hotly debated topics in science. Nobody can agree on what happened and when. One theory is that it started with gestures and sounds such as 'ouch' or 'eh', that evolved rapidly into something more meaningful. Observing vervet monkeys in the wild shows how a simple 'language' might develop. These monkeys have different alarm calls for particular predators. The call not only alerts the troop of danger, but also tells the monkeys what to do. The snake alarm call, for example, will see them all stand on their hind legs, looking for a predator on the ground. In response to the eagle alarm, they look up, drop from the trees and hide in the bushes, while the leopard alarm has them leaving the ground and clambering onto the thinnest branches in the trees.

Write it down

Long after language came writing. In western Asia and the Mediterranean it began about 5000 years ago in Uruk, where Sumerian scribes scratched marks on clay tablets as a means of recording the buying and selling of goods. Over time, different combinations of the marks came to represent syllables and words. This system of writing was used for thousands of years, until it was replaced by alphabet writing, such as that used by the ancient Greeks and Romans.

The printed word

People could communicate with many people at the same time after the development of printing. Although the German goldsmith Johannes Gutenberg is acknowledged to be the inventor of the printing press in the 15th century CE, printing occurred long before. In China, wood blocks with carved letters were pressed with ink and applied to paper from about 200 CE.

From prehistory to history

Writing marked the start of a new era in the story of humans. Before there was writing, useful information about life and living was probably passed from one generation to the next by word of mouth, with the danger it could be forgotten. With writing, it could be made more permanent. It also helped us to understand more about our past and learn from it. We had created history.

GROWING UP AS A HUMAN

Compared to the offspring of our closest primate relatives, human children grow up slowly and remain with the family for a long time. On average, females don't complete their transformation from girls to young women until they are 11 to 15 years old, and boys change even later. In contrast, young female bonobos reach maturity at five years old, and a year or so later will leave to join another group. One reason for the difference is the development of the human brain, which also had an impact on family life.

Late bloomers

As brains became larger and more complex, they required more energy, leading to young humans taking longer to grow up – twice as long as a young chimpanzee. This is most noticeable at five years old, when the brain receives most nutrients and is developing rapidly, but it is the period of slowest body growth. This means a longer childhood needing more parental care and an extended period in the protective setting of the home.
It prepares the brain of a child for the complex life of a human.

The human family

Your family might seem ordinary to you, but the human family unit is biologically unusual. Monkeys and chimpanzees live in larger groups, but we live in small, tight families in which we share our living space with only our closest relatives. In the west, the family unit is usually just parents and children, an arrangement that we share with gibbons, but with few other monkeys and apes.

LIVED TOGETHER, DIED TOGETHER

Family life does not fossilize so we do not know when humans started living in family groups. One early example comes from a village in Germany. At a 4,600-year-old burial site, an adult male and female with two boys have been found. They were lain down on their sides, facing each other, their arms intertwined, with their children between them. DNA analysis revealed they were a father and mother with their two children.

THE 'HOBBIT': OUR LAST COUSIN

While *Homo sapiens* was spreading across the world, a much smaller hominin was living at the same time on the Indonesian island of Flores. It was nicknamed the 'hobbit' on account of its short legs and big feet. Its small size is possibly the result of 'island dwarfism'. Animals isolated on islands over a long period of time with limited food and few predators tend to evolve to be smaller than their mainland relatives. The hobbit probably hunted dwarf elephants, which were small for the same reason. Scientists believe that this species, the Denisovans, and the Neanderthals may have been the last of our close cousins.

HOMO FLORESIENSIS

Pronounced: Ho-mo floor-es-ee-en-sis
Lived: Pleistocene epoch (100,000 to 50,000 years ago)
Size: 1.1 m tall

WHATEVER NEXT?

Although we can trace our ancestry back for millions of years, our species *Homo sapiens* has only been on the Earth for 300,000 years at the most. During that time we have changed rapidly from living in caves to living in space, and our impact on planet Earth has been immense, not all of it good. But, where do we go from here? Science fiction writers have often predicted that the humans of the future will have huge brains and little bodies, work alongside robots, and live on other planets. The reality will probably be something very different.

Is evolution over?

Some scientists think that human evolution stopped when we became modern *Homo sapiens*; after all, we can now control our environment. Natural predators, for example, no longer influence whether people survive or not. As one scientist put it: "Things have stopped getting better or worse for our species." However, other scientists believe our evolution has not stopped. As our population increases, the number of useful, random changes in our genes, known as mutations, increases too. New genes that boost our fitness and our ability to survive are appearing all the time. We may actually be evolving faster and faster, rather than not at all.

Shrinking brains

One of the surprising changes is that, even though our lives have been getting more complex, our brains have been getting smaller. This is because we're generally getting taller and have lighter skeletons as a species. Domestic animals have smaller brains than their wild relatives partly because they don't have to worry about hunting or foraging for food and escaping predators. Humans don't need to do any of those things either, so are we becoming domesticated too?

Population boom

About 10,000 years ago there were up to 10 million people on Earth. By the time of the Roman Empire there were 200 million. Today there are 7.6 billion, with the possibility of 11.2 billion in 2100. Such an increase raises a number of important questions. Where are we all going to live? How are we going to feed everyone? How do we live alongside the plants and animals of the natural world and protect our planet? These questions will become increasingly urgent for humans in the years ahead.

Science fiction or fact?

Scientists do not know how humans will evolve, but there are a few possible options. We might remain as we are, with a few minor changes, or a new species of human could evolve – either here on Earth or if we live on another planet. A third option is that human brains begin to work together with intelligent machines, and the human body disappears altogether. What do you think?

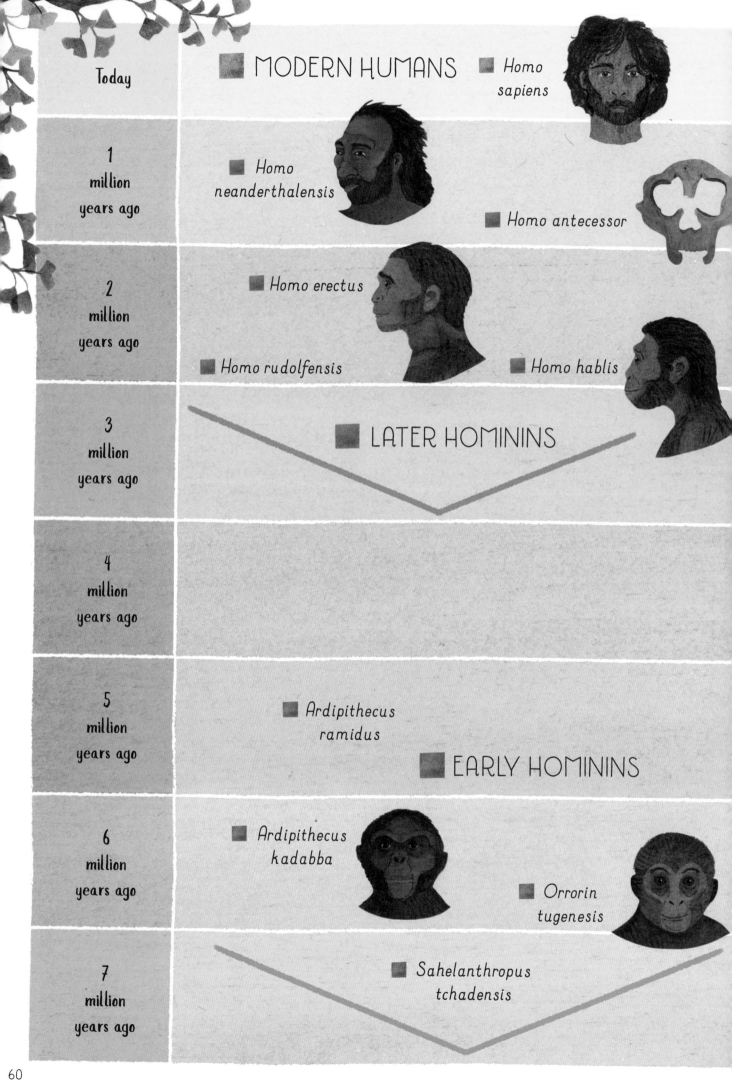

Today

MODERN HUMANS ■ *Homo sapiens*

1 million years ago

■ *Homo neanderthalensis*

■ *Homo antecessor*

2 million years ago

■ *Homo erectus*

■ *Homo rudolfensis*

■ *Homo hablis*

3 million years ago

■ LATER HOMININS

4 million years ago

5 million years ago

■ *Ardipithecus ramidus*

■ EARLY HOMININS

6 million years ago

■ *Ardipithecus kadabba*

■ *Orrorin tugenesis*

7 million years ago

■ *Sahelanthropus tchadensis*

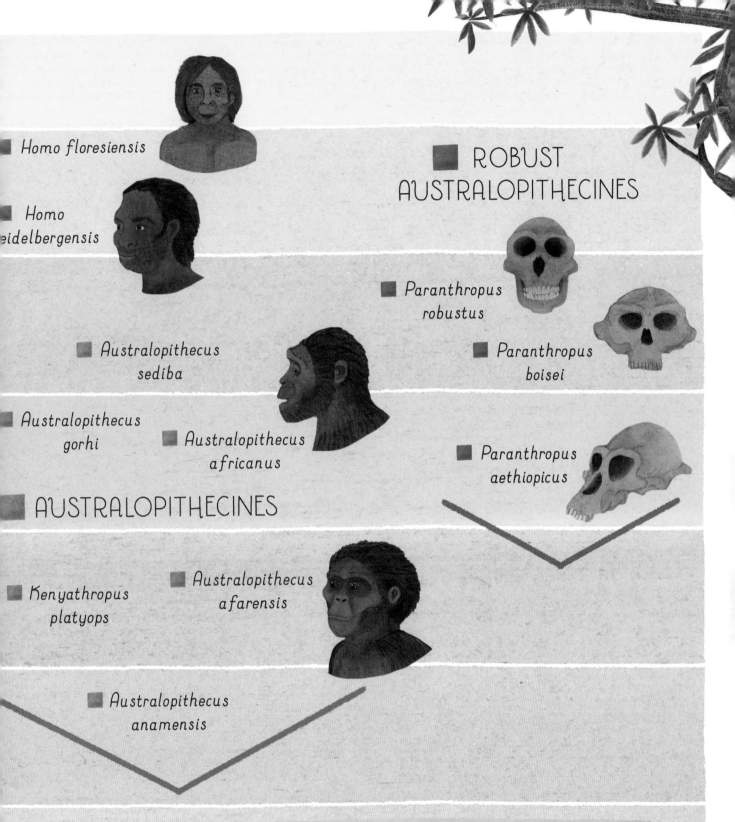

Homo floresiensis

Homo heidelbergensis

Australopithecus sediba

Australopithecus gorhi

Australopithecus africanus

AUSTRALOPITHECINES

Kenyathropus platyops

Australopithecus afarensis

Australopithecus anamensis

ROBUST AUSTRALOPITHECINES

Paranthropus robustus

Paranthropus boisei

Paranthropus aethiopicus

HUMAN FAMILY TREE

The epic story of humans has been long and complex. The family tree is not a neat straight line from one ancestor to the next, but one of many branches and frequent dead ends. The most recent chapter probably started in Africa and then spread to the rest of the world, and it features a cast of characters that constantly change as new discoveries are made. The only certain thing is that we – Homo sapiens – are the only surviving humans.

GLOBAL HUMANS

Homo sapiens was not the only hominin who migrated out of Africa.
As the map shows, several of our predecessors did too. While those heading for Europe
and Asia travelled mainly overland, those that reached the islands of the Indian and
Pacific oceans must have had boats. It shows the inventiveness of humans. It also reveals
how humans used that cleverness to conquer the world in less than 200,000 years.

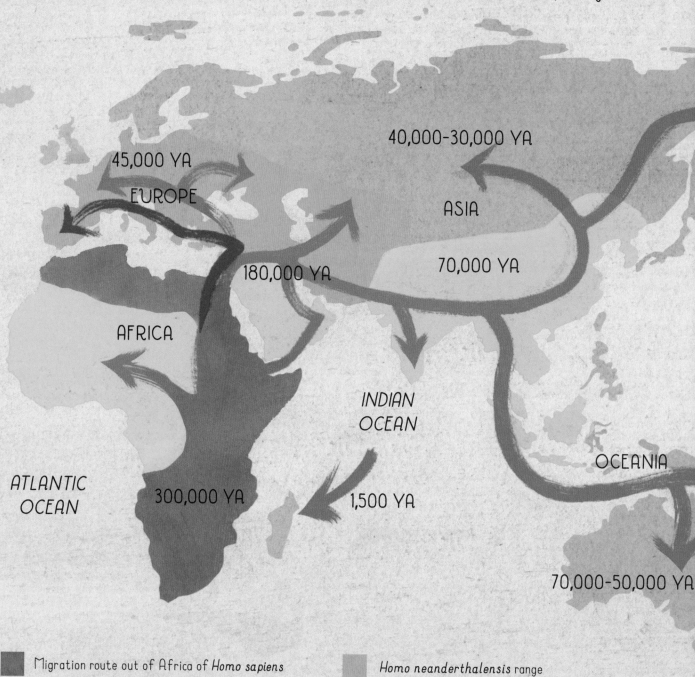

45,000 YA
EUROPE

40,000–30,000 YA

ASIA

180,000 YA

70,000 YA

AFRICA

INDIAN
OCEAN

OCEANIA

ATLANTIC
OCEAN

300,000 YA

1,500 YA

70,000–50,000 YA

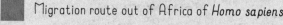

■ Migration route out of Africa of *Homo sapiens*

■ Possible migration route out of Africa of *Homo heidelbergensis*

■ *Homo neanderthalensis* range

Homo erectus range

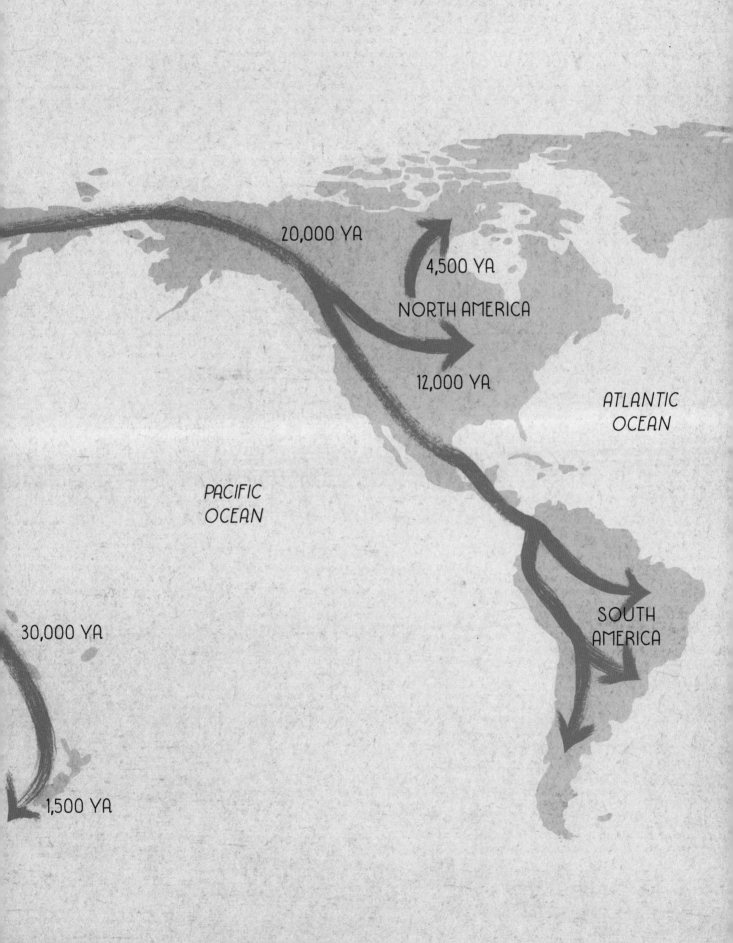

20,000 YA

4,500 YA

NORTH AMERICA

12,000 YA

ATLANTIC OCEAN

PACIFIC OCEAN

30,000 YA

SOUTH AMERICA

1,500 YA

INDEX